THE PRINCIPLE OF MOMENTS

Unique Perspectives on Leadership

Anthony J. Perkins

authorHOUSE®

AuthorHouse™
1663 Liberty Drive
Bloomington, IN 47403
www.authorhouse.com
Phone: 1 (800) 839-8640

© 2019 Anthony J. Perkins. All rights reserved.

No part of this book may be reproduced, stored in a retrieval system, or transmitted by any means without the written permission of the author.

Published by AuthorHouse 12/28/2018

ISBN: 978-1-5462-7400-1 (sc)
ISBN: 978-1-5462-7410-0 (e)

Print information available on the last page.

Any people depicted in stock imagery provided by Getty Images are models, and such images are being used for illustrative purposes only. Certain stock imagery © Getty Images.

This book is printed on acid-free paper.

Because of the dynamic nature of the Internet, any web addresses or links contained in this book may have changed since publication and may no longer be valid. The views expressed in this work are solely those of the author and do not necessarily reflect the views of the publisher, and the publisher hereby disclaims any responsibility for them.

This is an encouraging book that will challenge leaders
to reflect on their experiences and advance
their leadership to a higher level.

Enjoy!

This book is dedicated to the
children of St. Jude.
May God be with you on your journey.

Contents

Introduction xi

Raising Your Level 1
The Listening Leader 7
Yet, Here I Am 15
Heaven Only Knows 21
Digging Your Scene 29
Hungry like the Wolf 37
That was Yesterday 43
Give Us Attention 49
Finding Your Calling 55
Get off the Phone 61
Party of One 69
Fearless Leadership 75
Force or Fold? 81
Go the Distance 87
The 80/20 Concept 95
Slow Your Machine Down 103
Disappointment City 109
Stay Sharp 115
Hard Work is Hard 121
Setting a Daily Leadership Tone 127

About the Author 133

Introduction

Leadership consists of defining *moments*. You can define the *moments* or the *moments* will define you. It takes years to gain leadership credibility and only a moment to lose it. Leadership is a beautiful journey, yet many leaders take for granted the audaciousness to lead. Leaders have the authority, power, and influence to produce positive change. This is truly special. As a leader, it is your charge to make the organization better than it was the day before while instilling in your teammates that they have not seen anything yet.

There are many battles in leadership, including loneliness, doubt, anxiety, negative cultures, people that do not support you, and envy. Through perseverance and with a positive mindset, you can win these battles. To achieve a positive mindset, a leader's emotional state must be positive. This will lead to great actions and optimistic results. With a positive mindset—no matter the odds, a leader will succeed. Leaders who give up when the going gets tough do not realize how close they were to achieving their dreams, goals, and successes. Staying the course through the thick and thin, ebbs and flows, ups and downs, rejections, cant's, and what ifs, is essential.

This book, *The Principle of Moments: Unique Perspectives on Leadership*, consists of experiences from thirty-five years of leadership observations, successes, and failures. From these insights, readers can glean valuable leadership lessons to refine their own leadership styles.

RAISING YOUR LEVEL

Leaders, you are in leadership to be bold, to take risks, to survive challenges, to overcome obstacles, to beat the odds, to move forward, and to do things you never believed you could do. **You must convince the organization that they have not seen anything yet**. Leaders must have COURAGE! I see this as the number one leadership trait that is lacking in leaders. We have world, national, and local leaders who want to cruise through their leadership tenures. They are simply scared and do not want to make waves. They ignore the overall goal of making an impact. They tell one stakeholder one thing and another stakeholder another thing, while both stakeholders are left wondering what is true and what is not. Some leaders want to get paid a lot and do very little. Some want to remain comfortably neutral, to not have the truth associated with them. Others call their attorney to get advice, before turning around to say they can't do this or that per their attorney's instructions. Who is leading the organization? The leader or the attorney?

Shame on these so-called leaders. This is a perfect example of scaredy-cat leadership. Leadership is not about being reserved, stagnant, fearful, or deficient in confidence. It is about being audacious, sticking your neck out, working smart while working hard, and building a forward-moving culture.

To succeed, leaders must do things differently, stretch their limits, be uncommon, and expect more—of themselves and teammates. Leadership DNA necessitates having a will, drive, and hunger to outlast—a desire to stun, astound, and amaze teammates and customers. If someone asks you where Department A is within the organization, don't just tell them, *walk* them there. Show them the way; show them you care.

Have the courage to do the right thing even when it is not the popular option. People will notice your integrity and will respect your courage. Making decisions in contrast to your integrity (e.g., to keep your job) may work a few times but will only get you so far in your career. It's time for leaders to recommit to COURAGE as their defining characteristic.

Questions to Ponder:

1. How does the lack of courageous leadership upset the culture in an organization?
2. What does doing things differently, stretching your limits, being uncommon, and raising your level look like in leadership?
3. How do you teach your teammates to be courageous in their roles?

Notes

THE LISTENING LEADER

We have two ears and one mouth. This is a clue that we should be listening twice as much as we talk. Listening is the most important attribute in communication. Many of us spend 70–80% of our waking hours in some form of communication. Of that time spent communicating, about 9% is writing, 16% is reading, 30% is speaking, and 45% is listening. Studies confirm that most of us are poor and inefficient listeners. Therefore, it is critical that leaders are skilled in communication principles and techniques.

Even though listening is the communication skill that we use most frequently, it is also the skill for which we have had the least training. People have more formal training in writing, reading, and speaking. Another reason for poor listening skills is that we are able to think faster than someone else can speak. Most of us speak at the rate of about 125 words per minute. However, we have the mental capacity to understand someone speaking at 400 words per minute.

Studies have shown that, immediately after listening to a ten-minute oral presentation, the average listener has heard, understood, and retained 50% of what was said. Within 48 hours, that rate of retention drops another 50%, to a final level of 25%. This statistic confirms that we are inefficient listeners. Leaders and their teams can become better listeners by:

- ✓ Using a notepad or graphic organizer.
- ✓ Making mental summaries during pauses.
- ✓ Sitting up front.
- ✓ Being positive and open to the content of the message.

Leaders who are communicating a message can aid listeners' retention by:

- ✓ Ensuring the room is quiet.
- ✓ Offering a translator if necessary.
- ✓ Using a sound system if necessary.
- ✓ Utilizing alternative channels for presenting the message (e.g., projector screens, TV screens, headphones).
- ✓ Engaging the audience periodically with involvement activities.
- ✓ Confirming that communication is at the proper "level" for the audience.
- ✓ Using a method known as "The Power of 3," which calls for repeating information three times or more to help people connect with the message.
- ✓ Eliciting the participants to be active by having them do things during the event.
- ✓ Remembering that any lack of interest will depend on the listener's prior attitude toward the speaker, the content, and the implications of the message.

Leaders must also understand listeners' diverse cultural backgrounds. Failure to comprehend cultural backgrounds can be a major barrier to effective listening. Here are items to consider in cross-cultural communication:

- ✓ Proper voice tone.
- ✓ Interpretation of pauses and silence.
- ✓ Appropriateness of eye contact.
- ✓ Use of humor.

Leaders communicate to many people within and outside of the organization. This communication is conducted in various manners. Leaders should think about how they can get people to effectively listen to their messages. Much of the communication that leaders and teammates receive is oral; therefore, accurate listening is necessary for a valid understanding of what is being communicated.

Questions to Ponder:

1. Why is listening the most valuable attribute in communication?
2. Leaders communicate during most of the day, so how can they ensure listeners are retaining their messages?
3. After reading this section, what would you do differently when communicating?

Notes

YET, HERE I AM

There are many people who will challenge you during your leadership tenure. People will give you a hard time for many reasons, including ignorance, jealousy, misinformation, and prejudice, to name a few. Some people will even oppose you for doing the right thing, because the right thing is difference from their agenda. Demonstrating integrity in your leadership role is evidence that you are a mature leader with a focus on making things happen. As the saying goes, "You can do things right or you can do the right thing." What type of leader are you going to be?

As leaders, we are not exempt from the undesirable. The best leaders understand this comes with the territory and refuse to endure it. These leaders realize they must be problem solvers or the situation may allow such nonsense to be ignored with a focus on moving in a positive direction.

To know whether you are an effective leader, you need not wait around for your evaluation. You will know if you are effective because some team members will tell you, others will thank you for asking for their input, and several will appreciate that you included them on a collaboration. **But, most importantly, if you hear team members using your leadership language, this means they believe in you.**

When there are tough leadership *moments*, you must know these instances are temporary. Getting hung up on why these tough times occurred and who could have done this only prolongs the time it takes to get your organization moving in the right direction. If the cause of the problem is known, fix it.

Always be prepared and ready for both rewarding and perplexing times. There will be unexpected difficulties that come your way, but if you are well-prepared, no challenge is too great to overcome. As a leader, you can win your teammates over by building relationships with them. This does not mean you must become their best friend; make it clear that you care about them. Sit with them during training sessions, hold conversations with them during breaks, send them a note when they have birthdays, give them a gift when they welcome babies into their families, or appreciate them in public for doing a great job. Doing things like this in a genuine manner will break the ice between leaders and members of the team. By teaching, modeling, following through on promises, being present at functions, allowing teammates to shine, and going the extra mile, you will build credibility with your team. You want to be able to say with pride during your leadership tenure: "No matter what you throw at me, yet, here I am."

Questions to Ponder:

1. When ineffective leaders are identified, what specific professional development can be offered to improve their leadership capacity?
2. Your response to people who challenge you indicates your leadership maturity. What are some positive approaches to take when this occurs?
3. Recognizing your teammates, especially in public, is critical to boosting your team's morale. What are various methods to utilize in public to acknowledge your teammates?

Notes

HEAVEN ONLY KNOWS

Heaven only knows why many leaders practice "mean" leadership. Mean leadership is equal to death by a thousand paper cuts. Why do these leaders regularly exercise their authority in such rude and condescending ways? What drives them to think such an approach is positive and productive? How does this method motivate team members and advance the organization? The reason is, as humans, we do what we know. Mean leaders were trained that way, or they misinterpreted their leadership education.

Utilizing a mean leadership style produces little to no results, while causing a high turnover rate, a bad organizational culture, and a negative climate. Culture is defined as attitudes, expectations, and behaviors. Climate implies human interactions. The sad thing is, many of these mean leaders lead for many years before their negative leadership skills are identified and they are finally purged from the organization. Why does it take so long for bad leaders to be removed? The answer is that upper-level leadership fails to identify these leaders, or it condones their behavior. If upper-level leadership fails to recognize them, it is a function of poor oversight. If upper-level leadership condones mean leadership, however, it is because they do not understand how to lead people. These organizational leaders truly believe they are doing the right thing, yet everything they are doing is wrong. The result is failure in all areas of the organization.

One of the key factors in leadership is that organizations are only as great as their people. **Training, supporting, and inspiring your teammates will move your organization into greatness.** To be a leader who transforms an organization, you must effectively demonstrate qualities of collaboration, cultivation, preparation, a thirst for success, and, most importantly, courage. Teams that do not consistently meet these objectives often face dysfunction. You may be thinking this is all common sense, and that people should know better, but believe me when I say that mean leadership exists in many organizations. Remember: common sense is not necessarily common practice.

Case Study

Leader A has just completed a three-year tenure as the Chief Executive Officer of a school district. He would like to stay, and has been invited to continue as the district's leader, but he has not experienced enough support from the governing board and the community to move the school district forward. Both entities want to keep the status quo, which is mediocrity. Leader A is a leader who is truly focused on transforming things, always hungry for success and modeling his high expectations for others. Because he has not received support, he decides to resign and bring his drive and energy to another school district. What were Leader A's accomplishments? He built a strong foundation within the school district by reestablishing a culture of literacy in each school, technology was updated to assist with the teaching and learning process, and an active-learning teaching model was implemented to involve students in the instructional process.

There were other issues that needed attention, as well. This particular school district is very rural, making it difficult to recruit team members. To help with the recruitment process, a thirty-passenger shuttle was purchased to transport team members to and from the next town. Upon joining the school district, Leader A discovered that the district's high school had been closed for many years due to poor student enrollment. This meant students were being bused forty miles, one-way, to attend high school in the next town. Because of the long ride, many students dropped out of high school. Following Leader A's collaboration with many stakeholders, the high school was reopened with a charter-school organization leading all operations and instituting their own personnel. The charter school created an agreement between local government entities that involved no cost to the school district in exchange for the charter's use of the high school's facilities. This was a win-win solution, as students now had a local high school to attend instead of traveling eighty miles every day to attend classes.

After Leader A transitioned out of the school district, Leader B arrived and took charge. One of the golden rules in leadership is, *Before making major changes, learn the lay of the land within the organization*. During the first three to six months, a leader new to an organization should observe, ask questions, give a survey, and have discussions with team members. Exercising this patience will help new leaders discover what is working, what is not working, and what needs immediate attention.

What occurred next is an example of mean leadership. Leader B decided to close the high school, meaning students once again dropped out. So too did Leader B eliminate the thirty-passenger shuttle, forcing team members to find their own transportation to and from the schools, while also requiring teachers hired by Leader A to re-interview for their teaching jobs. How were these moves beneficial for the school district? This was not transformational leadership; it was mean leadership. This is one of many reasons why school districts struggle to advance in student achievement and organizational transformation. Was there any thought given to how these moves would impact students? Poor leadership is like poor parenting: in both cases, teammates and kids fail to grow.

Questions to Ponder:

1. How can interview teams be effective in identifying mean leadership styles during the interview process?
2. How can school leaders ensure that students remain the top priority when making decisions?
3. How can "learning the lay of the land" before making significant changes become a standard for all leaders?

Notes

DIGGING YOUR SCENE

Are your teammates "digging your scene" throughout your leadership tenure? Are you so inspiring that the team joins (not follows) you to exceed organizational goals? Are you organized? Do you utilize a collaborative leadership style? What are your cultivating strategies? Are you competent in your position? Do you dress in a professional way? Do you keep up with the latest research in your area of leadership? Do you treat teammates in a positive and respectful manner? What leadership skills do you employ to motivate associates to be passionate about their work?

It will take employees time to trust and respect you as a leader. Everyone has a degree of nervousness when new leadership arrives. The team is excited yet skeptical, wondering things like:

- Will leadership give me a chance to showcase my talents?
- What tools of support will leadership offer me?
- Can leadership teach or guide me to do well in my position?
- Is leadership knowledgeable?
- Can leadership truly move the organization forward in a collaborative manner?

Personnel will be quick to judge a leader. **Being sharp, collaborative, and a role model are traits that can immediately "ease the pain" of the team.** Do not implement any significant changes at first unless the situation is dire. Be patient, it will pay off. Work on your organizational culture first. What are the goals the organization needs to accomplish? Why does the organization exist—what is its mission? What does the organization aspire to be—what is its vision? Help paint this vision with your team. Remember, you lead at the level of your vision.

Questions to Ponder:

1. How do you want to be remembered during and after your leadership tenure?
2. In thinking about organizational vision, what facts (good or bad) will assist leaders and their teams in creating a realistic vision?
3. What are the attributes of a sharp leader?

Notes

Perk Up Quote

"Have more energy than the problem."

Anthony J. Perkins

HUNGRY LIKE THE WOLF

Do you want the crumbs or the cake with the icing? Being hungry in leadership is a necessity. *Hungry* does not mean having a cut-throat leadership approach, it means being prepared for an opportunity even while knowing one is not yet available. Imagine an animal stalking his prey and knowing it is about to eat a meal. That is what it means to be hungry for success.

In this regard, allow me to introduce you to Leslie Calvin "Les" Brown. Les is an American motivational speaker, author, radio DJ, former television host, and former politician. During Les's early years, he was hungry to be a radio DJ. He decided to go to the local radio station to speak with the station manager. The station manager walked into the room, and Les introduced himself and asked if there were any DJ openings. The station manager asked a series of questions, wondering whether Les had any experience. Les said he did not but emphasized that he was a quick study. The station manager told Les that there were no DJ positions available. Les thanked him and left. The next day, Les went back to the radio station and asked for the station manager. The station manager arrived, only to hear Les reintroduce himself. The station manager replied, "I know who you are, I just spoke to you yesterday. What part of *no* did you not understand?" To which Les responded: "I understand, sir, but you may have had someone quit, or maybe you had to lay someone off. I'm just checking." The station manager then angrily told Les to leave. The next day (the third day in a row) Les returned to the radio station and asked for the station manager. The station manager walked in very upset, and Les reintroduced himself and asked if there were any DJ openings. The station manager, bursting with annoyance, said, "Boy, go get me some coffee!"

Les now had his foot in the door at the radio station and was assigned to do various errands. Even though he was not yet a DJ, he started hanging out in the DJ booth to observe. One day, a DJ was drunk on the air, and the station manager, who was away from the station but still listening, called Les and asked him to call other DJs to replace the drunk DJ. Les said, "Yes sir, I will call around" and then hung up the phone without calling any DJs. Les waited approximately twenty minutes before calling the station manager to report that no one was available—but that he was ready to jump in. The station manager approved Les's request, and this event started Les's career as a DJ. His approach, clever and a bit deceptive but he reached his goal.

In a speech before a college audience, Les stated: **"It is better to be prepared and not have an opportunity than to have an opportunity and not be prepared."** Les's persistence paid off. There are many stories like this, where people were hungry to succeed and did so. Leaders must have the drive to never accept no for an answer, and they must understand that rejection is part of the leadership equation. Keep pushing when these *moments* occur.

Questions to Ponder:

1. How can "being hungry" be positive for a leader? How can it be negative?
2. How can leaders ensure they are prepared even though no opportunities are available?
3. How do leaders shift their mindsets to overcome rejection?

Notes

THAT WAS YESTERDAY

Do not dwell on the past; learn from previous leadership mistakes and victories and then move forward. Think of a vehicle. When you sit in the driver's seat, in front of you is the front windshield, allowing you to look forward and see far and wide. One could say this windshield provides a good view of things. Having this view allows you to make decisions and stay alert to various dangers in the road, while also knowing which way to go, being aware of pedestrians, and having the presence of mind to speed up or slow down.

Now imagine that you are still sitting in the driver's seat but have begun focusing on the two rearview mirrors located on the left and right exterior doors. Do you notice how small these mirrors are? This is because the driver should only use them quickly, to view items behind the vehicle. These mirrors represent the past. Visualize trying to use the rearview mirrors to drive the vehicle forward, and you will see it is impossible.

The analogy of the front windshield and the rearview mirrors applies to leadership. What is the leader's vision for his or her organization? Is it a far and wide (front windshield) vision, or is it a backward-looking (rearview mirrors) perspective? The takeaway from the past should always be that leaders learn from it and move forward, striving to continue doing great things while not making the same mistakes.

It has been said, "**The past is a place of reference, not a place of residence. The past is where we learned the lesson, the future is where we apply the lesson.**" Leaders, insert these quotes into your organizational beliefs. This will allow the organization to focus on the future.

Questions to Ponder:

1. In terms of leadership, how can dwelling on the past help and hurt an organization?
2. How do leaders lead with vision?
3. How do leaders empower their teams to focus on the vision?

Notes

GIVE US ATTENTION

If people are honest, they will admit to wanting some kind of attention during their careers. If they disagree, have them live a bit longer, and they will see how true this is. Attention can come in the form of appreciation, and it could be represented by a thank you, a pat on the back, a grateful email, praise during a team or public meeting, or a gift. **Attention is okay, but it can become a problem if we always seek it.** It is important for a leader to provide attention to his/her team. Why? Because hard work is hard. Taking the time to acknowledge team members is vital to creating a happy organizational culture.

Growth-mindset leaders understand the importance of taking time to embrace their teams. Teams that feel appreciated produce results and have an extra pep in their step. Once, there was an employee who received the EMPLOYEE OF THE MONTH award but only learned of this achievement when another employee saw the award posted in the breakroom. Upper leadership did not go to the employee's department to present the award in front of his colleagues. This is a true story. Say it ain't so! How do you think the associate felt? This is like leaving a Christmas gift in front of someone's house, instead of knocking on the door, handing it to him or her, and saying some kind words.

What can an effective leader do to appreciate and grow their team members? Start with understanding your teammates. What is their THING? For example, if you know some associates are into movies, buy them movie tickets. If some are into energy drinks, place an energy drink from time to time in their mailboxes. Others may collect stuffed animals, so perhaps you might buy a few and place them on their desks. Small symbols of appreciation go a long way. It is the simple things that show a leader truly cares. As Lynne Twist puts it, "What you appreciate—appreciates."

Questions to Ponder:

1. How can attention help and hurt an organization?
2. Why is it critical for leaders to take time to appreciate their teams?
3. What are additional methods, not yet mentioned, that leaders can utilize to show attention to their teammates?

Notes

FINDING *YOUR* CALLING

Leadership is a calling. A higher power has your journey mapped out, and it assigns you to lead people with a purpose and goal in mind. A calling could inspire a person to be the leader of a team that conquers cancer. Or a calling may involve a leader directing a team to improve the lives of children. Some people struggle with finding their calling in life. Some people debate this notion, but many experts agree that *everyone* has a calling. **Everyone is placed on this earth to contribute to the improvement of mankind.** Your calling is also known as your purpose. For those struggling to find their calling, here is some advice:

- Remove all the white noise in your life and listen carefully.
- Are you constantly thinking about a career? This could be your calling.
- Is *I know I should be doing* _____ *instead* something that you often find yourself thinking? This could be your calling.
- Do you sometimes think: *What would I do if I had no limits, no fear, and plenty of money?* This could be your calling. But note that you can achieve your calling without huge sums of money.

Many people are in leadership for the wrong reasons. They may be talented, but they lack leadership skills. They are simply thinking about a larger salary and do not realize how their poor leadership abilities hurt their teammates and the organization. They are oblivious to the bigger picture, failing to see what exists outside their own mindset. When it comes to leadership, leaders are going to earn every penny in their leadership role. The delusion in leadership is that a leader sits behind a desk, completes paperwork, and shouts out orders. Anyone can do this: it's called being a *manager*. Managers deal with the daily complexities of organizations. Managers, unless they build their capacity, are not ready for leadership. Leaders concentrate on visionary facets. A person called to a leadership role has an instinctive ability to troubleshoot and solve problems: a natural capacity to inspire associates.

Questions to Ponder:

1. What are variables that keep people from discovering their calling?
2. How can leaders support teammates to fulfill their career calling?
3. What do you think are the factors that account for such a small percentage of "true" leaders?

Notes

GET *OFF* THE PHONE

That's right, I said it: get *off* the phone. I am referring to your cell phone. Once, while I was speaking with another leader, his cell phone kept making various noises. You could tell the device was programed to make different sounds for texts, calls, and email messages. What was so rude about this encounter was that he repeatedly checked his cell phone during our entire conversation, as if failing to attend to the beeps and buzzes would cause the world to be overtaken by Dr. Evil.

As a leader, when you are in a conversation with another person, make your cell phone the least important object in the room. Make the other person feel like they are the most important thing in the room. Do not even look toward your phone when it rings. Keep your focus on the person in front of you. This will send a clear message that you respect their time and want to listen to them, emphasizing that they are important to you. There have been countless times that my cell phone rang, but I disregarded it. At times, people would stop our conversation and ask if I needed to take the call, but I told them they were more important to me and that I would attend to my cell phone later.

Studies prove that cell phones increase stress in the human body. One study suggests placing your cell phone outside of your bedroom overnight due to the light coming from the device. Both of these concerns cause the brain to be active, and they reduce our ability to have a great night's sleep.

Leaders, if you have a cell-phone attachment issue, return to making people the central focal point. Appreciate the *moments* with individuals, cherish those face-to-face interactions, and give people your undivided attention. The most precious gift you can give anyone is your time without any interruptions. Perhaps eliminating cell phones would encourage people to pay attention to one another, concentrate at meetings, and stay focused in vehicles. This may be laugh-worthy.

Questions to Ponder:

1. How can a cell phone be an effective tool in leadership? How can it be a harmful tool?
2. What are some methods leaders can utilize to make people feel important?
3. How can you successfully regulate cell phone usage within an organization?

Notes

Perk Up Quote

"The best leadership award is no award at all.
Leaders know in their hearts whether
they are making an impact."

Anthony J. Perkins

PARTY OF ONE

Leadership can be lonely. There will be many times when you feel like you are on an island by yourself and can see people moving about in the distance on the mainland. Why can leadership feel isolated? The answer is people. The leader must be sophisticated enough to be a significant part of his/her team while also making it clear that he/she is the leader. A leader's body of work must send a message that he/she is a role model, but also that there are policies and procedures to follow and goals to accomplish.

Followers struggle to understand leaders because they have not walked in the leaders' shoes. We judge leaders, and then when we become leaders ourselves, we understand why those individuals acted as they did at that time. Leaders work with numerous personalities on their teams, including some or all of the following:

- The always-late teammate.
- The aggressive teammate.
- The *I'm worth more than what you're paying me* teammate.
- The passive teammate.
- The jealous teammate.
- The *I want to do as little as possible* teammate.
- The *I know everything* teammate.
- The hardworking teammate.
- The sensitive teammate.
- The *I would have done it better, stronger, and faster* teammate.

A leader must be savvy enough to handle the various characteristics of people within the organization. It is necessary to understand and know how to approach various temperaments. For example, a leader must know how to motivate passive employees and must pull aside consistently late associates to let them know their behavior is unacceptable.

Leadership can be lonely at times, because the leader is the driver of goals, the hammer when necessary, and the visionary. However, the rewards of leadership are gratifying, particularly when a leader:

- Observes teammates growing professionally.
- Watches the beauty of people working together to become a true team.
- Transforms mindsets from fixed to growth.
- Achieves a victory.
- Knows that the team has made an impact.
- Inspires everyone to believe that the best is very close.

Just like a writer goes through a period of loneliness while writing his/her book, with the end result being a masterpiece that earns widespread recognition, leaders must go through lonely times to achieve team goals.

Questions to Ponder:

1. How can a leader balance loneliness with his or her need to be part of the team?
2. Why is it critical for leaders to understand their teammates?
3. How can it be damaging for leaders to isolate themselves from their teams?

Notes

FEARLESS LEADERSHIP

As a leader, you may be told to be fearless, to go out there and take names, believe you can do anything if you put your mind to it, or grab the bull by the horns. These are great words of encouragement but can be a challenge. People mean well with their advice, but they forget we are human. Leaders must understand that part of leadership entails having some fear. There will be many times when things go against a leader, which can instill fear. This is a normal human reaction, as unease and the unknown can cause distress.

Being entirely without fear in a leadership role is unrealistic, but it is possible to feel less fear. **The positive elements of fear are that it keeps leaders alert, helps them avoid trouble, maintains their focus, and has them ready to tackle *What if?* situations that might arise.** For example, what if customers are not happy? What if the project is not completed on time? What if the business deal does not go through? Whatever the case, as a leader, you must not allow fear to take control of your leadership. Fear can manifest from uneasiness and/or the unknown. If this is your mindset as a leader, you may not accomplish your goals. Leadership must comprehend that there will always be a *What if?*, but this should never impede organizational vision.

On a recent TV show called *Your Move with Andy Stanley*, Pastor Andy was given permission to talk about a current church member who is battling ALS (amyotrophic lateral sclerosis). ALS is a disease that eventually stops the muscles from functioning, and a common cause of death for ALS patients is when their throat muscles close and they can no longer breathe. The church member Pastor Andy spoke of is named Tim. Tim was at the pastor's home for a prayer group meeting and was asked to share life lessons regarding his fears while battling ALS. Here are Tim's profound statements:

1. "If you spend time with fearful people, you will adopt their fear." For example, if people are fearful regarding their leadership, looks, or finances, *you* will also have these fears.

2. "ALS makes everything I worried about in the past seem silly. Why do we continue to worry about everything? Stop worrying and live your life! The sooner people accept what can't be changed, the easier it becomes. Some people in the ALS community put all their energy into fighting, striving, and denying, rather than living. They are disappointed in the end." As humans, we believe that most things we worry about are important, but, really, they are irrelevant.

3. "It is the fear of the unknown . . . but the truth is, very little is really unknown, because at the end of ALS is death."

How can leaders overcome fear?

- Adopt an attitude of faith (i.e., I believe I can), not fear.
- Stay prepared so you do not have to get prepared all over again.
- Just do it. Jump in and LEAD.

Leaders, please stop saying: "It is what it is." This is a fear statement. This means you are giving in to what is average, ordinary, and mediocre. Instead, say: "It is what I *make* it." Then, you will have control over your fears.

Credits: *Your Move with Andy Stanley* (August 18, 2018). Andy Stanley-Fearless.

Questions to Ponder:

1. How can leaders have less fear?
2. What were some of Tim's overall points within his profound statements?
3. How can a leader train his or her team to overcome fear?

Notes

FORCE OR FOLD?

When the pressure is on, you want people to see you as a leader with force not as a leader who folds. **A leader with force is a leader who inspires, motivates, makes things happen, beats the odds, does not have time for excuses, overcomes barriers, and constantly pushes his or her team toward excellence.** You want to be a positive force not a negative force in leadership. You want your team to state that you were a positive force in getting things accomplished: a "make it happen" leader.

In order for leaders to be a force, they must have knowledge and skills. They must be able to lead and to endure what their team is going through. It is critical for leaders to have walked in the footsteps of their teammates. They cannot be effective Chief Executive Officers (CEOs) if they have not successfully completed associate tasks related to the organization's mission. Leaders may struggle as CEOs if they do not have the relevant educational background. Knowledge and skills give leaders credibility. Going up the organizational ladder properly, without skipping positions, is key. For example, how can a school district superintendent lead if he or she has not been a successful school teacher, principal, and district director? Leaders cannot lead what they do not know. Too often you discover leaders who are in a hurry to climb the organizational ladder and who want to bypass positions. If this practice is allowed in an organization, these leaders find themselves struggling to lead and move their teams. To become a leader with force, leaders must learn and earn.

Questions to Ponder:

1. How can a leader be a positive force in leadership?
2. How can using negative force in leadership be harmful to the organization?
3. How can learning and earning be effective components for leaders?

Notes

GO THE DISTANCE

You will go through growth phases during your leadership journey. Understand that this is normal, and do not let the unknown make you nervous. Think about life in general: we face the unknown every day. Do we panic at this realization? No, we get up and go about our lives. As things unknown arise, we accept them and calmly move forward. The same can apply to leadership. Expect that there will be unknowns, and then accept them, tackle them, and move forward.

Sometimes anxiety or stress can take over your mind. **Switch from negative forecasting to positive forecasting, meaning you will convey a mindset that most of your leadership will involve positivity, but there will also be a dose of negativity from time to time**. Inserting positive forecasting into your mindset will help you through your leadership season.

Your goal as a leader is to evolve. Every year, you should refine your strengths and address your weaknesses. Below are possible phases of your leadership journey:

- <u>Years 1–4 (Phase I)</u>: Building Your Capacity

During these years, you will face a learning curve. It is critical for you to absorb all of the knowledge and skills available to you. However, you should not wait for people to give you anything. You must seek out learning opportunities. Surround yourself with strong leaders who will share wise advice and who will be a role model for you. In this phase, learning is key. Even when you have acquired much knowledge, you still have much to learn. Your team will understand that you are building your capacity during this phase, but they will expect more from you at its conclusion.

- ❖ <u>Years 5–8 (Phase II)</u>: Discipline

For the duration of this phase, you must be disciplined in order to apply your new knowledge and skills. Take what you have learned and utilize these traits by applying, analyzing, evaluating, and creating within your organization.

- ❖ <u>Years 9–12 (Phase III)</u>: Coaching

Over the course of these years, your knowledge and skills should be at a higher level as compared to your early leadership years. If you have truly increased your capacity and remained disciplined while applying your knowledge and skills, you are now in a position to coach your teammates. You can now give effective feedback and model behavior for them. Your associates will expect this from you now that you have reached a higher level of leadership. Remember though, while you have much to offer, you still have a lot to learn. Always look for avenues and opportunities to build your capacity.

- ❖ <u>Years 13+ (Phase IV)</u>: Mentoring

At the thirteenth year and beyond, you are now in a position to mentor new or less experienced personnel. You are able to successfully guide and lead others. This is an honor. Be humble in this role, and be grateful you have achieved a level of expertise wherein you can share your knowledge and skills. It is important to give back as much as possible during this phase. The next generation of leaders need to be polished and ready in order to take on the challenges of tomorrow. To do well in this phase, you must have completed the first three phases at a high level. The mistake some leaders make in this phase is that they get too comfortable or cocky. They feel they have earned the right to be lazy and to cruise into retirement. This is poor thinking. This is your time to motivate and teach teammates. In a leadership role, you should always be excited and ready to lead. You should always share your knowledge and skills. To reiterate: be grateful, give back, and always be humble. As Maya Angelou stated, "When you learn, teach. When you get, give." And, as Booker T. Washington put it, "If you want to lift yourself up, lift up someone else."

Questions to Ponder:

1. What are effective methods for leaders and their teammates to utilize in order to handle the unknowns?
2. How can leaders shift their mindsets to become positive forecasters?
3. What are the key components to being successful in all four phases?

Notes

THE 80/20 CONCEPT

When it comes to your diet, the best approach is to eat healthy 80% of the time, giving you 20% of the time to eat whatever you would like. When it comes to exercise, 80% of your time should be spent being active and 20% relaxing. Think about this 80/20 split in terms of leadership. As a leader, expect that 80% of your day, week, month, and year—what you have planned—will be accomplished. However, you should also anticipate that 20% of your leadership vision may not come to fruition.

Too many leaders expect perfection during their leadership tenure. Perfection is an ambitious aspiration, but it is unrealistic. Do not stress over trying to be picture-perfect. As long as 80% or more of your leadership expectations are being met, be grateful. However, this does not mean leaders cannot push organizational successes to higher levels, perhaps achieving 90% success. The 80/20 concept suggests that things should run smoothly 80% of the time (or more), but you should expect a glitch in the matrix from time to time. There will be barriers to overcome, unseen roadblocks, and many other obstacles. For example, there may be upset customers, personnel may not be taking care of business, there may be a facilities issue, and so on.

Remember, relationships do not always work out, vehicles do not work all the time, and our kids are never perfect. So, why would we expect our leaders to be flawless? Understand that there are many stakeholders within the organization who contribute to it with different philosophies, values, and beliefs. It is the leader's job to have everyone join him/her for a shared vision. Educate your team on giving their best effort 100% of the time. Everyone must give 100% every minute of every day, however, 20% of the time things may not work out. **Do not stress over failures, shortcomings, or mishaps. Instead, overcome, adapt, or improvise.** Ensure that misfortunes are within the 20% range. If they tend to be higher, conduct an analysis of systems and the people leading them.

Questions to Ponder:

1. How can a leader ensure an 80% or higher success rate within the organization?
2. How can leaders help their teams handle the 20% concern?
3. How do leaders handle hardships that arise more than 20% of the time?

Notes

Perk Up Quote

"Be an unrealistic thinker."

Jim Calhoun

SLOW *YOUR* MACHINE DOWN

Stop the go, go, go, and be more of a slow, slow, slow leader. Being a "slow leader" does not mean leading at a snail's pace; it means going slow so that, when it's time to go, you are ready. Slow down to listen, learn, take notes, research, and build your capacity. Slowing down as a leader supports a more innovative and creative mindset. It gives the leader time to thoroughly analyze and create.

Multitasking can cause a leader to make mistakes. We have all tried to juggle many tasks in the past only to miss a detail or forget something. Focusing on one task and completing it to the fullest is a more beneficial approach. The likelihood of details being missed and things being forgotten is slim to none.

It is important to take time to absorb life going on around you. Appreciate the beautiful *moments*, the wins, the barriers that were broken, the limits that were shattered, and all of the times that your organization was victorious when the odds and people suggested that it would not. Take time to smell the leadership roses.

During the initial stage of practicing a slow leadership approach, leaders will be tempted to revert to their normal practices. Resist this urge and stay the course. Soon the slow approach will become the norm. Leaders will find this approach to be less stressful and more fulfilling, with results they can own. To help with the initial stage of slowing down, leaders must change their inner dialogue; then, their actions will follow.

Remember, when you find yourself moving too quickly—ask yourself, What's the rush? Where's the fire? The saying "Speed kills" can be valid in leadership, if you allow it. Practice and stay disciplined to go slow in order to be a go-go leader.

Questions to Ponder:

1. What are the consequences of leaders moving too fast?
2. How can leaders stay disciplined to maintain a slow leadership approach?
3. What are the benefits of a slow leadership approach?

Notes

DISAPPOINTMENT CITY

Leadership will include disappointing *moments*. There will be team members who will let you down, people will play politics at the office, you may get passed over for a promotion, or there will be some customers who simply want to find something bad about the organization. Unfortunately, there will be unfair situations.

As the saying goes, "Disappointments are inevitable, but misery is optional." It is important to understand that, while disappointments may arise, letting those disappointments fester—letting a negative feeling or problem become worse or more intense, especially in the long term—is not a wise practice. Accept disappointments and work quickly to remedy them. Leaders will endure many punches, but they must avoid the knockout blow. When those punches occur, leaders must pick themselves up and continue the good fight. Remember, leadership is not about the leader; it is about the end result. The result may be a project that makes a significant impact in the lives of many people. Now *that* is worth taking on some punches.

Novice leaders have a tendency to take a disappointment from small to big quickly. Instead, leaders, you should take a breath and be thankful for the positives that have already occurred in your organization. Take an optimistic approach to handling all situations. As a leader, it is crucial that you train your team to expect disappointments and handle them effectively.

Leaders, convert a disappointment into an opportunity for the future. **Having a mindset of fresh possibilities after a disappointment can remove the anger and negative thinking.** This is similar to losing a girlfriend and thinking you will never find a better one, only to find a new girlfriend that is awesome and ten times better than your last one.

Questions to Ponder:

1. What are methods to overcome organizational disappointments?
2. How can leaders train teammates to handle disappointments?
3. What are the benefits of "fresh-possibilities" thinking after a disappointment?

Notes

****STAY SHARP****

No one likes a dull pencil. Writing with one makes a document appear dismal. Sure, you can read the content, but you don't get a sharp, precise impression. In the same spirit, if leaders are dull, uninspiring, inapt at motivating, or unable to transform an organization, not only will that leave a dismal impression, the leader will not be in charge for long.

Sharp leaders have many solutions to problems. Sharp leaders are very competent. Sharp leaders cultivate their teammates. Sharp leaders are disciplined. Sharp leaders are humble. This is a tall order for many leaders, but, through effort, will, and focus, they can become proficient within these dimensions. What do these qualities look like?

- A sharp leader has many solutions to a problem. Leaders must approach a problem from various angles. Remember, to reach a destination, one can travel the popular route, or one can take different routes. The same applies to solving problems.
- A sharp leader is very competent. It is important to study, research, observe, and shadow strong leaders. In order to be competent, a leader must be well-prepared. Not only should a leader be book-smart, he or she also needs to be people-smart. A leader's competence should stand out.
- A sharp leader cultivates his or her teammates. A leader can be critical or cultivating. Cultivating leaders yield high results. If leaders want their associates to meet organizational goals with enthusiasm, they should nurture, support, and promote their teammates. There is no need to be

overly critical in a leadership role. Be a leader who teaches and nurtures.
- A sharp leader is disciplined. Discipline is not only what you do, it is also what you do *not* do. Stay focused on the task at hand. Leaders must not be lured away from their goals by a concept that is untested or that seems too good to be true.
- A sharp leader is humble. Leaders must appreciate and understand the blessing within leadership. This is the leader's time to push the team's performance to a higher level. This is the time to make things happen. Humble leaders put the organization's mission and vision, as well as their own teammates, before anything else. Humble leaders understand that it is not all about them.

Stay sharp. You can do this!

Questions to Ponder:

1. Why is it important to be a sharp leader?
2. What separates a dull leader from a sharp leader?
3. How would you teach a teammate to become a sharp leader?

Notes

HARD WORK IS HARD

Where sports umpires are always looking for mistakes, leaders are always trouble-shooting. It is easy to trouble-shoot when a leader has experience. Leadership is not for the faint of heart. Leaders must make tough decisions. They must take strong stances, deliver bad news, and endure what their teams endure. Effective leaders roll up their sleeves and join their teams in accomplishing tasks instead of sitting behind a desk and shouting out orders.

Leadership is hard because of the long hours it takes to produce greatness. Leadership is hard because success is not convenient. Leadership is hard because things may be smooth one minute, but could begin to crumble the next minute. Leadership is hard because there will always be some type of negativity that creeps into a gap within the organizational culture. Leadership is hard because of the multitude of responsibilities that can become overwhelming. Leadership is hard because great results are not only expected, they are demanded.

If "hard" is not expected from a leader, when "hard" happens, the leader will feel as if he or she has just been hit with a brick. Expecting hard circumstances from time to time will soften the blow. **Expecting hard times is not negative thinking. It is actually smart and forward thinking. Smart leaders accept that there will be hard situations during their leadership tenure.**

Expecting challenges is vital to excelling in a leadership role. Leaders who are prepared, who think in positive ways, who have more energy than the problem, and who know they can beat the issue will succeed. Leaders, be the leader who tackles hard work! Be the leader who handles your business!

Questions to Ponder:

1. How can hard work help a leader grow?
2. Why should a leader expect challenges from time to time?
3. What are the differences between a leader who is prepared for hard work and a leader who is not?

Notes

SETTING A DAILY LEADERSHIP TONE

Many people get up in the morning and sip from a cup of coffee to set the tone and draw energy for the day. This notion can also apply to leadership. When waking up in the morning, leaders should immediately set a positive tone for their leadership day.

A best practice for leaders is to surround themselves with positivity. What does this look like? Leaders can turn on soothing sounds, such as classical music, jazz, or any other type of music that puts their minds in a positive state. The music must be relaxing and joyful to the leader. Leaders can also take in positive programming on the radio, computer, or television, inspiring themselves to be optimistic. Leaders can incorporate jogging or exercise in the morning to get a runner's high and to get blood pumping throughout the body. Meditation in the mornings can help a leader stay focused and sharp during the day. The list of HOW TO START A LEADER'S DAY IN A POSITIVE MANNER is endless. Leaders know what stimulates them. Selecting and utilizing methods every day helps leaders set a positive tone for the day.

Delving into social media or following the morning news is not a positive path for leaders. Why? These platforms are negative, adversely affecting leaders as they seek a more positive mindset. It is important for a leader to explore many purposeful get-up-and-go energetic morning routines.

Leaders should research other successful leaders to discover their daily routines or unique traditions. A leader never knows what they will learn when they explore.

Questions to Ponder:

1. What are things you can do in the mornings to set a positive daily leadership tone?
2. What approaches can hurt a leader when setting a daily leadership tone?
3. Why is setting a positive daily leadership tone important?

Notes

About the Author

Dr. Anthony J. Perkins was born and raised in Connecticut. He presently resides in Buckeye, Arizona. In 2018 he began his twenty-fifth year as an educational leader, a career in which he has served as a teacher, vice principal, principal, district director, and now superintendent for the Gila Bend Unified School District. He holds a master's degree in education, with an emphasis on diverse learners, and a doctoral degree in educational leadership. His dissertation is titled *Breaking the Hispanic Dilemma: Familial Factors that Contribute to Academically Successful Hispanic Students.* In addition to his school experience, Dr. Perkins is a mentor for new school principals, and he teaches educational leadership classes for Northern Arizona University. Dr. Perkins's personal interests include physical fitness, golf, and jazz music. However, he enjoys spending most of his time with his beautiful daughter.

If you wish to follow him, you can find him on Facebook as Dr. Anthony J. Perkins. You can also email him at: perkup67@yahoo.com. He thanks you for your support and asks you to continue to make people smile.

www.ingramcontent.com/pod-product-compliance
Lightning Source LLC
Chambersburg PA
CBHW030757180526
45163CB00003B/1061